Disasters in
Space Exploration

DISASTERS

IN

SPACE EXPLORATION

Gregory L. Vogt

The Millbrook Press
Brookfield, Connecticut

Library of Congress Cataloging-in-Publication Data
Vogt, Gregory.
Disasters in space exploration / Gregory L. Vogt.
p. cm.
Includes index.
ISBN 0-7613-1920-4 (lib. bdg.)
1. Space vehicle accidents—Juvenile literature. [1. Space vehicle accidents.]
I. Title.
TL867 .V64 2001
363.12'4—dc21   00-069189

Cover photograph courtesy of AP/Wide World Photos
Photographs courtesy of Sovfoto/Eastfoto: pp. 9, 14, 22, 23, 41; NASA: pp.
18–19, 26, 30, 35, 39, 42, 45 (both), 49 (both), 52, 53, 57, 59, 63; Photo
Researchers, Inc.: pp. 16 (Geoff Tompkinson/SPL), 24 (NASA), 25
(NASA/SPL), 56 (NASA/SPL); Jim Oberg: pp. 31, 36, 46; AP/Wide World
Photos: pp. 34, 54

Published by The Millbrook Press, Inc.
2 Old New Milford Road
Brookfield, Connecticut 06804
www.millbrookpress.com

Contents

Introduction

AND THEN THERE WERE WOLVES

Alexei and Pavel felt a sharp jerk
as their parachute snapped open. Their
Voskhod 2 space capsule descended
quickly to the snowy land. Trees from the
forests of the western Ural Mountains
reached up to receive the bell-shaped
capsule. At the last possible moment,
small retrorocket engines in the
capsule fired, cushioning the impact.
They were going to make it after all.

The word *voskhod* means "sunrise" in Russian, and the men inside the Soviet capsule were cosmonauts Alexei Leonov and Pavel Belyayev. Both men had been in space just the day before and made history. Their mission was difficult. They accomplished things that no one else had, but the mission nearly killed them. Alexei and Pavel were lucky to be alive.

The flight of *Voskhod 2* began on March 18, 1965. Only eight years before, the space age had begun with the launch of the world's first artificial satellite. The first human to fly into space began his trip only four years before. The United States and the Soviet Union were locked in a race to see which one would conquer space first. That meant being the first nation to send humans to the Moon and bring them back safely.

The Soviets were in the lead. They launched the first satellite into space, the first animal, the first human, and the first space capsule to carry more than one human. The U.S. space program was coming in a poor second. Many of its rockets failed to reach space, much less orbit Earth. Still, the National Aeronautics and Space Administration (NASA) was learning quickly. Each launch improved on the previous ones. Eventually, the United States took the lead and, in July 1969, set two men on the surface of the Moon. But the pathway to the Moon was dangerous and, for some, deadly.

During the flight of the *Voskhod 2*, Alexei and Pavel added another Soviet first: Alexei became the first human to venture outside a space capsule and "walk" in space. To make this happen, the *Voskhod* space capsule had to be redesigned. At this time, the Soviets employed vacuum-tube technology for its instruments. Opening the door of the space capsule and exposing hot vacuum tubes to the vacuum of outer space would lead to overheating and invite disaster. An airlock was added to the capsule.

The idea of the airlock was simple. Instead of just one door, there were two. Once in space, a double wall tube of fabric would be inflated, pushing the outer door away from the capsule. The tube was 8.25 feet (2.5 meters) long and 3.6 feet (1.2 meters) in diameter. The space walker would slip into the tube and close the inner door behind. After draining the air from the tube into space, the outer door would be opened, and the space walk could begin.

8

Alexei Leonov (left)
and Pavel Belyayev
inside *Voskhod 2*

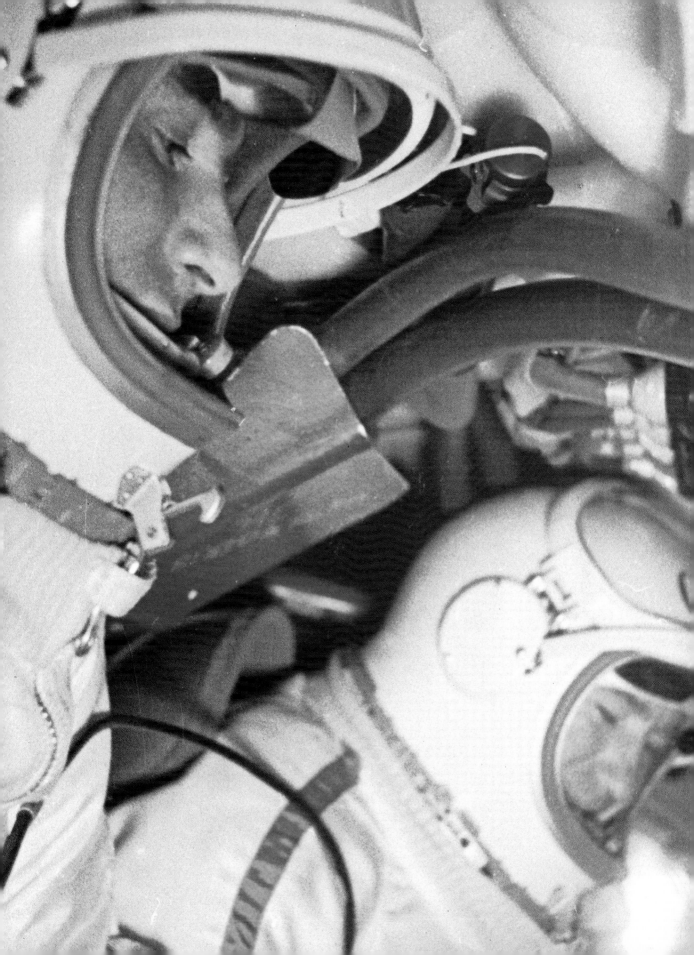

The previous October, three cosmonauts had roared into space in *Voskhod 1*. The mission was successful, and the crew returned safely. The capsule was a tight fit for the three cosmonauts. To do a space walk meant that the astronaut going outside would have to wear a protective garment, a space suit. Adding a space suit onboard the *Voskhod* would take up too much room for three people. One astronaut had to be cut from the mission.

Alexei Leonov was chosen for the space walk. He wriggled into an uncomfortable space suit made out of tough fabric and a helmet with a clear face visor. Air was pumped inside the suit to keep him alive, and additional layers inside the suit protected him from temperature extremes in space.

Leonov slipped outside the airlock and made space history. He tumbled about at the end of an umbilical line. The line became twisted, and Alexei struggled to unwind it. In only a few minutes it was time to return to the safety of the capsule. Alexei made a frightening discovery. His suit had ballooned up too much for him to bend his legs and reenter the tube. As Alexei struggled, his heart and breathing rate soared. Pavel, inside *Voskhod 2*, couldn't see what was happening and was unable to come to Alexei's aid. All he could do was listen to Alexei on the radio saying, "I can't…I can't get in." Failure to return to the capsule would mean certain and excruciating death for Alexei. He would be the first person to space walk and the first person to die on a space walk—all in the same few minutes.

Alexei finally released some of the life-giving air from his suit, and the suit softened enough so that he could bend his legs. He slipped back through the tube to the safety of *Voskhod 2*. It was a close call but not the last for the mission.

The next day, the rocket crew attempted to fire braking rockets to begin the reentry process. The rockets failed to fire. Without the rockets to slow them, Alexei and Pavel could not return to Earth. They would breathe away their oxygen supply and suffocate.

The designers of the spacecraft planned for that contingency and built a backup retrorocket system into the capsule. These engines did fire, and reentry began. The delay caused the capsule to land 2,000 miles (3,220 kilometers) away from their planned landing site. The recovery crews were in the wrong place.

Alexei and Pavel opened the hatch of their capsule. It was late winter in the Ural Mountains, and the air was very cold. The two lonely cosmonauts built a fire to keep warm. They waited for a recovery crew to arrive the next morning. The fire felt good, but the light attracted a pack of wolves that circled the cosmonauts in the darkness. Alexei and Pavel decided it would be best to wait inside their capsule. There, shivering the night away, they watched the wolves as the wolves watched them. The next morning, ski troops rescued the space heroes.

Chapter 1

Out of This World

Ask any astronaut or cosmonaut. He will tell you that traveling through space is the most exciting, thrilling, and fun thing that he has ever done. Ask any astronaut or cosmonaut. She will tell you that traveling through space is the most dangerous thing that she has ever done.

Soviet cosmonaut Svetlana Savitskaya making repairs to the space station *Salyut 7*, July 25, 1984

Outer space is a thrilling but alien environment. You have never experienced anything like it, and if you ever do, you will die. The scientists, engineers, and mission controllers, who launch people off Earth, go to great lengths to make sure those people are not exposed to outer space. They build spaceships and space suits to isolate the space travelers. These devices are shells that surround the travelers with a bit of Earth's environment.

No Home Away from Home

Outer space has several important properties that make it quite different from the environment of Earth. First, outer space is a vacuum. That is why it is called space. There is no air. Earth's dense atmosphere of nitrogen and oxygen, held to the planet by Earth's gravity, thins out the higher up you go. About 100 miles (160 kilometers) up, there is so little air that you will die in seconds if unprotected. Air will flood out of your lungs. You can't hold your breath. The pressure inside your lungs would be too great.

Without air, your skin begins to swell. Humans evolved on the surface of Earth where the air pressure at sea level is 14.7 pounds per square inch (101 kilopascals). Every bit of skin and every nook and cranny on the human body is squeezed by air. It accumulates into tons of pressure.

In space, that pressure is gone. Body fluids begin to boil. Bubbles form in the bloodstream and in the water contained in the cells of the skin. The skin inflates. The fingers of the hands will expand to the size of knockwurst. It will be painful.

In addition to the body swelling, lack of pressure will cause the eardrums to rupture outward to release the air contained in the inner ears. The bubbles in the bloodstream will eventually block the veins in the brain, leading to a

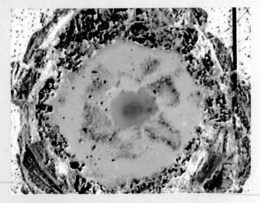

A colored light-micrograph of an impact crater caused by space junk on a solar panel of the Hubble Space Telescope. Space junk is the term for man-made waste in space.

cerebral hemorrhage and death. It will be over in about 15 to 30 seconds.

The body will be exposed to temperature extremes, high-speed particles, and dangerous radiation. The side of the body facing the Sun will sizzle at temperatures up to 350 degrees Fahrenheit (176 degrees Celsius). The side in shadow will cool down to a shattering -250 degrees Fahrenheit (-156 degrees Celsius). Tiny bits of comets and asteroids will strike at speeds of dozens of miles per second. In time, the body will be pitted with tiny meteorite craters. The dangerous radiation won't affect the body much because the damage to body cells occurs too slowly to make a difference.

Fortunately, for astronauts and cosmonauts, spacecraft and space suits provide ample short-term protection from outer space. However, being in outer space is not the only danger facing them. There is danger in getting to outer space, and there is danger in returning to Earth.

Vertical Flying Machines

To get to outer space, all you have to do is go up. That sounds easy, but the technology to reach space has been known only for about 50 years. Before traveling into space, people first learned to fly. More than 200 years ago, the first human fliers were hot-air balloonists. About 110 years ago, humans rode kitelike gliders. Almost 100 years ago, the first human made a flight aboard a powered and controllable airplane. With each technological development, there was a price to be paid. The early fliers had to fight against gravity to remain in the air, and sometimes they lost. In spite of the dangers, safe air travel has become commonplace for millions of people every day. Traveling to outer space, however, is a problem of an entirely different magnitude of difficulty.

Since space has no appreciable amounts of air, the wings of airplanes won't provide any lift for spacecraft attempting to orbit Earth. Propellers, helicopter rotors, and jet engines won't work either. The only way to get to space is with rockets.

In principle, rockets are simple vehicles. Rocket fuel, carried inside the rocket, is burned in one or more engines at the rocket's lower end. High-speed flames and rapidly expanding superheated gases jet out the engines' nozzles. This provides thrust to propel the rocket upward. A payload consisting of a satellite, human passengers, or spacecraft traveling to other planets is carried at or near the rocket's top.

Though simple-sounding, the technology to do this is staggering. Even to have a chance of reaching space, the rocket has to weigh as little as possible. It has to carry all its fuel. The oxygen needed to burn the fuel in the vacuum of space is contained inside the fuel itself. In a launch vehicle like NASA's Space Shuttle, more than 10 tons of highly explosive fuel is consumed every second for the first part of the trip. The exhaust flames from the engines are hot enough to melt rock.

Depending on the rocket, hundreds of thousands or even millions of parts have to function perfectly. Starting at zero miles per hour, the rocket climbs on a pillar of flame hundreds of feet long and reaches outer space in less than 10 minutes. To remain in space, when the fuel runs out, the payload has to be traveling at 17,500 miles (28,160 kilometers) per hour. That is nine times faster than a rifle bullet.

If the payload is human passengers, the spacecraft has to provide air, pressure, moderate temperatures, water, food, waste removal, maneuverability, and a place and the tools to do work.

Following a stay in space of a few days, weeks, or months, the space trav-

elers have to return to Earth. Getting back is another of the dangers faced. The space vehicle first has to slow down by a few hundred feet per second to begin the reentry process. Small rocket engines accomplish the slowing when they are fired in the direction the vehicle is traveling in orbit. Putting on the brakes in space changes the shape of the orbit to a spiraling fall. It is important that the fall not be too steep, or the vehicle will slam into the upper

A test firing of the QM-6, the third redesign of the Space Shuttle solid rocket motor. Extensive redesign and testing were necessary after Space Shuttle 51L exploded during liftoff. (See page 50 for the story.)

atmosphere and disintegrate in the intense heat generated by friction with the air. If the path is too shallow, the vehicle could skip off the atmosphere and head back into space like a stone skipping off water.

If all goes well, the space vehicle with the travelers inside returns safely to Earth. Parachutes bring space capsules down to the ocean or land. Wings enable the Space Shuttle orbiter to land on a runway.

Chapter 2

MAGNIFICENT SPACE MACHINES

Having the power to reach outer space is only half the problem with space travel. When you get there, how do you survive, and how do you get back? The answer is a special flying machine called a spacecraft. Spacecraft come in two basic shapes but in a range of sizes. The shapes are determined by how you plan to return to Earth's surface. The size is determined by the power of the launch vehicle and how many other people and pieces of equipment you want to take with you.

Yuri Gagarin inside
the *Vostok 1*

In the early days of manned spaceflight, rockets were barely powerful enough to reach space and achieve the speeds needed to orbit Earth (about 5 miles, or 8 kilometers, per second). The first spacecraft were capsules in which single astronauts or cosmonauts were stuffed inside. Cosmonaut Yuri Gagarin rode a heavy-duty sphere or cabin and an instrument module on the bottom. The vehicle was called *Vostok 1* ("East") and weighed about 10,000 pounds (4,540 kilograms). When Gagarin returned to Earth after just one orbit, the instrument module was discarded, and the capsule burned its way through the upper atmosphere. A heat shield on the bottom side of the capsule protected Gagarin. About 2 miles (3.2 kilometers) above the ground, Gagarin ejected from the capsule and parachuted the rest of the way down.

The Americans went to space in a bell-shaped *Mercury* capsule that had a rocket escape tower attached to its upper end. The escape rockets would be used only during launch to pull the capsule away from the rocket if there was a problem. If everything went fine, the tower would be ditched before the capsule reached space. The weight of the capsule and tower was about 17,500 pounds (7,940 kilograms). For reentry, the blunt end of the capsule was aimed into the airflow so that the heat shield could protect the single astronaut inside. Parachutes slowed the capsule so that it could make a gentle landing in the ocean.

Improvements in the *Vostok* led the Soviet space designers to build the two-person *Voskhod* ("Sunrise") spacecraft. One of the major improvements was a parachute and retrorocket system for setting down the capsule on land with the astronauts inside. Parachutes alone would lead to a rough landing. Just before landing, small rockets would fire, producing a cushioning blast for the final touchdown. Later Soviet space capsules took on the bell-shape

The fairing is put on the lower portion of *Voskhod*. This outer shell protects the spacecraft from the high temperatures of takeoff. The fairing is shed in space, where it becomes space junk. Earth missions have generated a fair amount of space junk.

first used by the United States. The *Soyuz* ("Union") was a three-part vehicle. It featured the bell-shaped reentry vehicle but had an instrument module attached to its broad end and a spherical orbital capsule to its narrow end. The orbital capsule gave the three-person crew inside more space to live and work.

The United States continued its spacecraft development with the two-person *Gemini*. Though larger than *Mercury*, the *Gemini* was still a tight fit because it had to hold two astronauts. The *Gemini* did not have the escape tower. Instead, emergencies would be handled by an ejection and parachute system. The *Gemini* had an instrument module attached to its broad end, which was ejected for reentry, and it also landed by parachute in the ocean.

Walter M. Schirra (left) and Thomas P. Stafford in the *Gemini IV* capsule

The *Apollo 11* capsule awaiting recovery. The crew, wearing isolation suits, was transferred to a mobile quarantine unit on the U.S.S. *Hornet,* where they remained for 21 days.

The largest U.S. capsule was the *Apollo.* It was planned for the Moon flights but was later used for ferrying astronauts to the *Skylab* space station and during the *Apollo-Soyuz* mission. Three astronauts rode the capsule into orbit. It was attached to a service module along its blunt end. The service module provided oxygen, water, and power to the capsule. For the Moon-landing missions, a boxy two-stage lander was added to the flight. The lander had four legs that would open and a large rocket engine for a soft touchdown on the Moon. The upper part of the lander had its own engine that carried the Moon walkers and their Moon rocks back to orbit to rejoin the command and service module. Back on Earth, only the command module would survive reentry and parachute to the ocean for splashdown.

Gus Grissom's *Mercury 4* capsule, which he named *Liberty Bell 7*, was too heavy for the helicopter to lift. The capsule was cut loose and sank in deep water.

LIBERTY BELL 7

One would think that if you were going to sacrifice your life for space travel, you might meet a spectacular end. Virgil "Gus" Grissom nearly drowned! Grissom was the second American astronaut to travel into space. His flight was virtually a repeat of Alan Shepard Jr.'s flight a few months before. Grissom rode a *Mercury* space capsule on top of a Redstone rocket. He was pitched up in a suborbital path that carried him into space for only a few minutes before plopping him into the Atlantic Ocean about 15 minutes later.

Everything had gone well until Grissom's capsule, which he named *Liberty Bell 7*, splashed down in the Atlantic Ocean. While waiting for a helicopter to pick up the capsule and set it down on the deck of an aircraft carrier, the side hatch of the capsule suddenly blew open. Water began pouring into the capsule. Grissom scrambled out the hatch as *Liberty Bell 7* began sinking.

In his hurry to get free of the capsule, Grissom did not remember to close the oxygen port of his space suit. Water began seeping into the suit as air escaped from the neck of the suit. Grissom began treading water as hard as he could as his suit got heavier and heavier. Fortunately, the recovery helicopter was able to get a sling down to Grissom before he followed *Liberty Bell 7* to the bottom.

The Space Shuttle

The Space Shuttle is unique among space vehicles. It was designed by NASA for routine space travel. All other space vehicles (except the Soviet shuttle look-alike *Buran* that reached space unmanned only once before being retired) return to Earth with a parachute system.

The Space Shuttle is a true spaceship. It consists of four parts: the delta-winged orbiter, a brownish external tank, and two solid-rocket boosters.

The crew rides in the nose of the orbiter in a cabin that looks like the cockpit of a commercial jetliner. Payload is carried in the back of the orbiter in a cavity that is 60 feet long (18.2 meters) and 15 feet (4.6 meters) in diameter. The orbiter itself is 122 feet (37 meters) long, and the wingspan is 78 feet (24 meters).

At liftoff, the orbiter is pointing nose straight up. It is attached to the external tank, and the boosters are attached to the side of the tank. Liquid hydrogen and oxygen are sucked into three main engines in the orbiter's tail at a rate that would drain a good-size swimming pool in just 25 seconds. When the engines reach their full thrust, the solid-rocket booster kicks in, and the Shuttle is airborne.

Two minutes after liftoff, the boosters empty and drop off to parachute into the Atlantic Ocean. Ships retrieve them for later use.

Chapter 3

CARNAGE AND CLOSE CALLS

The space age began with the technology of warfare. Powerful rockets were needed to reach the edge of space. Even more power was needed to place a satellite or spacecraft into orbit. Still more power was needed to send space probes and astronauts to the Moon. The technology to accomplish these aims was already well under development when the United States and the Soviet Union each decided to embark on space travel.

A Soviet missile test in 1960. Photographs of the Soviet space program are not easy to come by because the country was in direct competition with the United States in the race for space, and space technology often came directly from top-secret military technology. Photographs of Soviet space program disasters are even harder to find, because the Soviets had a habit of covering up mishaps, even to the point of editing dead or disgraced cosmonauts out of photographs.

Large missiles were constructed by Germany to carry warheads across the English Channel during World War II. The missiles, called V2s, approached the edge of space and then fell back to Earth to explode on impact in London. At the end of the war, many V2s were captured and brought to the United States along with top German rocket scientists and technicians. The Soviet Union got its share of the missile experts too. Experiments with the missiles marked the beginning of the space age.

During many test launches small scientific payloads were carried instead of warheads. The experience gained from the launches began to pay off. Gradually, many improvements were made in rocket technology. Rockets became capable of spaceflight. The first rockets to carry satellites and humans

This V2 rocket is not German; it is American. After World War II, the United States worked hard to recruit German rocket scientists who continued their missile program in the United States with hardly any time wasted.

into orbit were intercontinental ballistic missiles. Yuri Gagarin rode a *Vostok 1* missile and orbited Earth one time on April 12, 1961. Alan Shepard Jr. rode a Redstone missile to space and dropped back down after a 15-minute ride. John Glenn Jr. flew on an Atlas missile and orbited Earth four times. Many satellites and space probes today are still launched with modified missiles.

In spite of the experience gained in launching hundreds of missiles, launch crews still had lots of trouble getting successful flights. Rockets are quirky machines, and things often go wrong.

Launchpad Conflagration

In the fall of 1960, three years after the Soviet Union launched *Sputnik*, the world's first artificial satellite, something terrible happened. The space race was running hard, and shortcuts were occasionally taken. A powerful intercontinental ballistic missile was perched on a Siberian launchpad. Before it could be launched, the missile developed a fuel leak that had to be closed. Normally, the procedure for making such a repair required "safeing" the vehicle. In other words, the fuel would be removed before repairs were started.

The launch was under the control of Field Marshal Mitrofan Ivanovich Nedelin. He ordered engineers and technicians out to the pad to make the repairs immediately without "safeing" the missile. Apparently, Nedelin had little understanding or respect for the technology he was commanding. The Soviet space program had recently lost two spacecraft sent to Mars, and a new space spectacular was needed to impress the world. Nedelin didn't want to lose any more time in launching the rocket.

The launchpad workers scrambled over the steel gantry structure that surrounded the rocket. There was a problem the next morning 30 minutes before the missile was scheduled to be launched but there is some disagreement on exactly what happened. A technician either pulled out an electronic component or plugged one into the rocket's second stage. The second stage ignited in a fireball that bathed the gantry in 5,400-degree Fahrenheit (2,980-degree Celsius) heat.

After years of secrecy, one of the survivors told the story in a weekly magazine. "At the moment of the explosion I was about 30 meters [100 feet] from the base of the rocket. A thick stream of fire unexpectedly burst forth, covering everyone around. Part of the military contingent and testers instinctively tried to flee from the danger zone, people ran to the side of the other pad, toward the bunker." The witness told how a newly laid strip of tar immediately melted. "Many got stuck in the hot sticky mass and became victims of the fire." People on the upper part of the gantry were so heated that they "burst into flames like candles blazing in mid-air." Approximately 100 people, including Field Marshal Nedelin, were killed as the entire missile exploded.

An Emergency That Never Was

John Glenn became the first American to orbit Earth, on February 20, 1962. He traveled to space in a tiny *Mercury* capsule mounted on the top of a silvery metal Air Force missile called the Atlas. The rocket performed as planned, and in minutes Glenn was traveling in a slightly egg-shaped orbit as high as 162 miles and as low as 141 miles (260 and 227 kilometers) over Earth. Every second, Glenn covered a distance of 5 miles (8 kilometers).

As Glenn began his second orbit of Earth, the capsule's autopilot system began acting up. Control jets started and stopped on their own, and the capsule began a slow turn. Eventually, Glenn had to disengage the system and control the spacecraft himself. It was important upon return that the capsule enter the atmosphere with its blunt end downward. Glenn would have to steer it himself. Then another problem happened.

An indicator light at Mercury Control began flashing. The light warned that the heat shield on the capsule bottom might be coming loose. The landing system for the *Mercury* capsule consisted of the heat shield and a heavy rubber landing bag. After doing its job, the shield would be dropped, and the accordionlike landing bag would fill with air. It would serve as a shock absorber for splashdown into the ocean. If the shield came loose, the capsule would be exposed to the tremendous heat of reentry, and Glenn would be incinerated.

When Glenn began his reentry, he was instructed to leave the retrorocket pack on the bottom of the capsule in place. Controllers believed the straps for the pack would help the heat shield remain in place and protect Glenn. Burning the retropack during reentry provided Glenn with quite a light show as he descended. On cue, his parachutes opened, and Glenn safely splashed down into the ocean.

As it turned out, the indicator light had given a false signal, and the precautions for reentry were unnecessary. The important thing was that Glenn was safe.

John Glenn being helped from *Friendship 7* by the crew of the U.S.S. *Noa.* Glenn's capsule landed 44 miles (71 kilometers) from the primary recovery ship. *Noa* was closest and made the recovery.

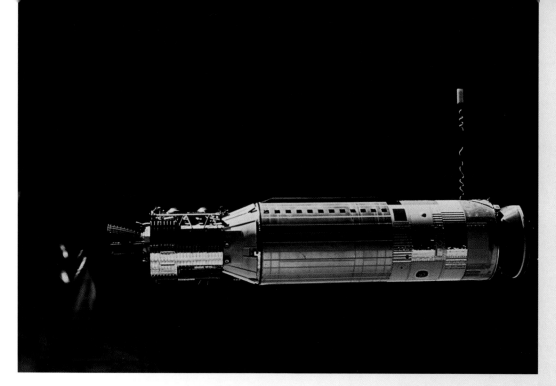

The *Agena* was used for docking exercises with *Gemini 8*.

Wild Ride

Neil Armstrong nearly missed his opportunity to be the first human to set foot on the Moon. One of the critical operations of a Moon landing was the rendezvous and docking of a spacecraft. Along with David R. Scott, Armstrong practiced that very maneuver on the *Gemini* 8 mission in 1966.

Armstrong and Scott's *Gemini* capsule easily rendezvoused with an unmanned *Agena* satellite that had been launched the day before. Armstrong guided the capsule forward until the two spacecraft docked. Everything was going well until about a half-hour after the docking. Armstrong had been directing the attitude-control system on the *Agena* to fire when, suddenly, the two crafts began to twist and roll. The crew didn't know what the problem was, but they assumed the *Agena* was at fault since the attitude-control system of the *Gemini* was turned off for the tests. They shut off the *Agena* system, and Armstrong brought the two spacecraft under control. Then the tumbling began again, only much worse.

Armstrong wrestled the spacecraft back into a stable mode again and then initiated undocking. That should have solved the problem. It didn't. The problem was actually with the *Gemini*. A thruster was firing continuously, and it was bleeding down much-needed attitude-control propellant. By now, the capsule was spinning at 60 revolutions per minute. Much faster and the crew would pass out. Armstrong used the thrusters for the reentry control system to stop the spinning. It worked. Mission Control had them cut their mission short, and the two splashed down safely in the Pacific Ocean.

Later *Gemini* flights had improved controls for their thrusters. Each thruster had an individual switch to shut it off if it should run wild again.

Oxygen Under Pressure

Materials that do not burn under ordinary conditions ignite under pressure. In 1962, Valentin Bondarenko, a 24-year-old Soviet cosmonaut, was undergoing a routine training exercise inside a pressure chamber. The chamber was filled with pure oxygen gas.

Valentin Bondarenko

Bondarenko had completed some medical tests and began cleaning spots on his skin where sensors had been attached. He used a small piece of cotton soaked in alcohol. In a moment of carelessness, Bondarenko tossed the soaked cotton aside. By terrible chance, the cotton landed on a hotplate. The heat from the plate ignited the cotton, and young Bondarenko quickly became engulfed in flames as his flight suit ignited.

A doctor, supervising the test, immediately tried to open the chamber. The increased gas pressure inside the chamber made the door impossible to open. A pressure-relief valve had to be opened and the extra pressure bled out of the chamber. It took several minutes to get the door open. Bondarenko was still alive and mumbled, "It was my fault, no one else is to blame...." The cosmonaut had burns over his entire body except the soles of his feet. Those had been protected by his boots. Bondarenko somehow remained alive for 16 hours.

The Bondarenko tragedy was kept a secret by the Soviet space program for many years. James Oberg, an American expert on the Soviet space program, has suggested that keeping the secret was costly. Had the managers of the American space program known of the tragedy, they might have recognized in time the dangerous situation created by placing three astronauts in a space capsule filled with pure oxygen at sea-level pressure.

Apollo 1

The race to the Moon was going hot and heavy. Everyone expected that it was just a matter of months before someone was going to land on the Moon. It was anyone's guess whether it would be an American or a Russian.

January 27, 1967. It had been a long day. The first *Apollo* crew was nearing the completion of another launch simulation. They were reclining inside their *Apollo* space capsule on top of an unfueled Saturn 1B rocket. Virgil "Gus" Grissom, Edward H. White, and Roger B. Chaffee were each wearing space suits. The tests they were conducting were part of a long series of tests to become familiar with the *Apollo* capsule and rehearse the things they would do during flight.

Two decisions, made earlier, led to disastrous consequences. A company, North American Rockwell, was given the contract for constructing the capsule. Rockwell's engineers argued that the atmosphere in the capsule should consist of oxygen and nitrogen like the atmosphere of Earth. They also wanted to have explosive bolts for opening the hatch in an emergency. NASA did not agree. An oxygen and nitrogen atmosphere would be hard to maintain, and if too much nitrogen would be released into the cabin, the astronauts would not be aware of the problem and would get sleepy and die.

Oxygen had been used safely in the *Mercury* and *Gemini* capsules, and NASA decided to go ahead and use it in the *Apollo*. The explosive hatch issue was also decided against Rockwell. Grissom insisted that the hatch on the *Liberty Bell 7* triggered on its own. Rockwell engineers believed that Grissom somehow must have accidentally triggered the hatch. Regardless, if the hatch on the *Apollo* were to trigger in space and the crew were not wearing their space suits, the crew would die in seconds. The explosive bolt hatch was replaced with a manual opening hatch that opened into the capsule.

The crew had been working their way through a long checklist and was pausing for a communication problem to be solved. The cabin atmosphere contained pure oxygen and was pressurized to 16.7 psi (115 kilopascals), 2 pounds above sea-level pressure.

Grissom was heard to say on the COM link: "Hey!" Chaffee then came on the line and said, "There's a fire in here!" Test crews outside the capsule went into immediate action and tried to open the hatch. The heat from the rapidly growing fire increased the cabin pressure even more, causing the inward-opening hatch to seal more tightly. Even under ordinary conditions, opening the hatch would take 90 seconds. Now, it was next to impossible to open. The rescue crew struggled for several minutes as dense smoke was building up. Five and a half minutes after the fire started, the situation was brought under control. It was too late for the crew. Doctors later determined that Grissom, Chaffee, and White died from breathing toxic gases rather than from the burns they received. The heat from the fire had melted through the suits. Grissom's and White's suits were actually fused together.

The cause of the fire was determined to be a spark from some wiring. In a pure oxygen, high-pressure environment, things burn that wouldn't normally burn. A piece of paper ignites like a torch. Although the technical cause of the fire had been established, the real cause was believed by many to be the haste to get to the Moon first. Shortcuts were taken, and normal safety precautions were of secondary importance. Donald Slayton, a former *Mercury* astronaut, said: "We got in too much of a ... hurry!" Manned Flight Director

The charred *Apollo 1* capsule

Kris Kraft said: "We were willing to put up with a lot of poor hardware and poor preparation in order to try to get on with the job, and a lot of us knew we were doing that."

The Apollo program shut down for two years while the *Apollo* capsule was redesigned and the program to go to the Moon was restructured. Never again would the capsule be flooded with oxygen at sea-level pressure. Better and less flammable materials were installed inside the capsule to cut the fire risk. The hatch was made to open outward.

Sudden Impact

Three months following the *Apollo 1* disaster, the Soviet *Soyuz 1* thundered off the pad. Inside the capsule was Colonel Vladimir M. Komarov. He had been the commander of the first *Voskhod* mission three years earlier. His *Soyuz* vehicle consisted of three components: a cylindrical propulsion and instrument module, a bell-shaped reentry vehicle, and a spherical orbital module.

Komarov's flight was to be the start of an orbital feat that would supposedly accomplish the same space objectives that the U.S. *Gemini* program took 10 flights to do. Three more cosmonauts in *Soyuz 2* were scheduled to follow Komarov into orbit so that the two space vehicles could rendezvous and dock. It was not to be.

Soyuz 1 began having trouble right after launch. Solar panels that were to open like wings and provide electrical power from sunlight did not work right. One of the panels failed to open. Without sufficient electrical power, the thruster system for controlling the vehicle began malfunctioning. Komarov struggled to keep the spacecraft from tumbling. He was ordered to return to Earth as soon as possible.

Komarov was unable to stabilize the *Soyuz* for retrofire during his first two reentry attempts during the sixteenth and seventeenth orbits. Without a steady burn of the braking rockets, he couldn't slow his vehicle enough to come down in a controlled fashion. Komarov finally succeeded in achieving

Vladimir M. Komarov

retrofire during orbit eighteen, but the burn was imprecise. The reentry capsule came down in a steeper and faster path than planned. It became unstable, and the main parachute lines became tangled. Komarov deployed the emergency chute, but it became fouled with the first chute. Komarov was helpless as his capsule plummeted toward Earth. In his last moments of life, Komarov watched Earth reach up for him. The capsule hit the ground like a boulder at a speed exceeding 300 miles (480 kilometers) per hour!

Apollo 13

They were 200,000 miles (321,800 kilometers) from Earth. Riding inside the *Apollo Odyssey* command and service module and attached to the *Aquarius* lunar module, the crew of *Apollo 13* were having an uneventful trip to the Moon. James A. Lovell, John L. Swigert Jr, and Fred W. Haise Jr. had just completed a television broadcast to the American people back on Earth. The crew didn't realize that the national television networks were uninterested in the transmission and were unwilling to interrupt regular television programs to show it. Shortly after the program, seen only by the people in mission control and the astronauts' families, the crew began some housekeeping activities.

One maintenance job required Swigert to operate electric stirring rods inside the four tanks holding liquid oxygen under extremely low temperatures. The oxygen was used for breathing, making electric power, and propulsion. Sixteen seconds after the stirring began, there was a bang, and the

After jettisoning *Odyssey*, the *Apollo 13* service module, the crew in *Aquarius*, the lunar module, could clearly see damage from the explosion—an entire panel had been blown off.

whole space vehicle shuddered. Alarms began going off inside the spacecraft, and the crew was mystified as to what had happened. Swigert radioed to mission control in Houston. "Hey, we've got a problem here." Lovell had to repeat Swigert's message. "Houston, we've had a problem."

As power systems on the spacecraft began failing, the astronauts ran through their checklists and tried to figure out what had happened. Could a meteoroid have struck them? A meteoroid the size of a grain of sand would strike with a force equivalent to being walloped by a bowling ball at 60 miles (100 kilometers) per hour! Looking out the windows, they saw debris outside the spacecraft and gas venting away. Oxygen levels were dropping. It was later determined that a defective heater inside one of the oxygen tanks caused the oxygen to expand, overpressurizing the tank and causing the tank to explode.

Working with the crews at mission control on Earth, the *Apollo 13* astronauts shut down as many systems as they could on *Odyssey* to conserve power for an emergency return to Earth. They moved into the *Aquarius* lander and used it as a "lifeboat." The timing of the explosion was bad. The crew could not turn the spacecraft around and head back for Earth. They would use up almost all their fuel just stopping the forward momentum of the spacecraft and wouldn't have enough fuel to start the home trip. They would have to continue on to the Moon and use the Moon's gravity to bend their course in a circle to swing back toward Earth.

For the next several days, the crew shivered in misery. The inside of the spacecraft became very cold, their breaths fogged, and water condensed into ice on the windows. Food had to be eaten cold. There was no place to get comfortable. Gradually, their breathing air began to go bad. Carbon dioxide was building up. The *Aquarius* was designed for two astronauts, not three. Its oxygen-cleansing system could not handle the breathing of three astronauts. Normally, the system on *Odyssey* would take care of the carbon dioxide, but it was shut down to conserve power. The cleansing-system canisters from *Odyssey* would not fit the system on *Aquarius*. Eventually, with the help of engineers on Earth, a device was rigged up that used parts from both systems to clean out the poisonous carbon dioxide.

Apollo 13 wasn't out of trouble yet. The astronauts still had a long voyage home. It was important not only to get home, but also to reach home at the proper angle. If the spacecraft reentered Earth's atmosphere too steeply, it would burn up. Too shallow, and the vehicle would bounce out again. Since the service module with the main rocket engine was out of commission, the crew had to use the descent engine of *Aquarius* to make several maneuvers. One took place the day after the explosion to readjust their speed so that they would swing around the Moon once. A second engine burn gave them a strong kick in the proper direction to head them back. Just under 180,000 miles (289,620 kilometers) from Earth, a third burn had to be made. The spaceship was drifting off course, and a correction had to be made to get them back down the center of the corridor. The crew had to fire the engine at 10 percent throttle for fourteen seconds in exactly the right direction.

Aquarius was not equipped for this kind of maneuver, and the crew had to improvise. No autopilot for the burn was available. The crew had to do it manually. Swigert became the timekeeper. Lovell handled ignition and shutdown and the roll and pitch controls. Haise took care of the yaw control. Controlling the direction was tricky, but they did it. *Apollo 13* was running straight and smooth.

Six days after liftoff, the crew scrambled back into their command module. In spite of all the water condensation and the shutdown of several days, the module came to life on the battery power that was carefully conserved for it. They jettisoned *Aquarius* and the service module. Three tired, cold, hungry, and thirsty astronauts were safely recovered from the Pacific Ocean.

Three More Lost

Following the U.S. success in landing astronauts on the Moon, the Soviet space program sought another mission in space to achieve greatness. On April 19, 1971, the world's first space station was sent into orbit. It was called *Salyut 1*. The station reached orbit ten years and a week after Yuri Gagarin

Donald K. Slayton, director of flight crew operations, explains to officials of the NASA Manned Spaceflight Center how a lithium hydroxide canister connected to a space suit exhaust hose will remove carbon dioxide from the air of the *Apollo 13* command module. The device, nicknamed "the mailbox," was duplicated on *Apollo 13*.

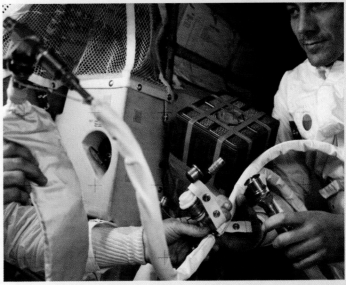

John L. Swigert assembling the hose for "the mailbox" assembled on *Apollo 13*

became the first human to reach space. The name of the station meant "salute" to Gagarin.

The idea behind the station was that it would be an orbital home for cosmonauts who would rocket into orbit in *Soyuz* spacecraft. They would dock with the station and remain in space for weeks or months, where they could do scientific research in the microgravity environment found there. They could study Earth below and the heavens above. The U.S. space program had been planning for a space station to follow the *Apollo* Moon missions, but it was two years off.

Four days after the station launch, the first crew to the station lifted off in *Soyuz 10*. The system for docking to *Salyut* was new, and the crew failed to join with the station. A second *Soyuz* crew was successful in docking on June 6. Cosmonauts Georgi Dobrovolsky, Vladislav Volkov, and Viktor Patsayev lived and worked on *Salyut 1* for 23 days. They conducted biomedical studies in space and broke the record for the most days in orbit.

On June 29, 1971, the crew returned to Earth. Disaster struck. A pressure-relief valve opened prematurely when the descent module separated from the rest of the *Soyuz*. Viktor Patsayev frantically tried to close the valve but was unable to do so. Being a tight fit for three cosmonauts, there wasn't any room for space suits. The cabin air immediately flooded out into space. When the recovery crew opened the capsule hatch, the three cosmonauts were dead.

Like the U.S. program after *Apollo 1*, redesign of the *Soyuz* spacecraft kept Soviet cosmonauts on the ground for two years. From then on, all cosmonauts would wear space suits inside their space capsules during critical maneuvers.

Disaster Averted

The *Apollo* Moon missions were over. Except for the excitement of *Apollo 11* and the close call for *Apollo 13*, the American public was losing interest in space exploration. NASA's quest to be first, fastest, highest, and longest no longer held the public's enthusiasm after the goal of reaching the Moon was achieved. Regardless, NASA forged on and launched *Skylab*. It was the first U.S. space station and by then the only one in orbit. While the Soviets retooled their program, the orbit of *Salyut 1* decayed, and the space station reentered the atmosphere and disintegrated.

Skylab took advantage of the hardware for the *Apollo* Moon program. The launch vehicle was the *Saturn 5*, and the rocket's third stage was modified to become the space station. The plan was to have two large winglike solar panels open from the sides of the station once it reached orbit. Four more panels, resembling the blades of a windmill, would also open from one end of the station. *Skylab* would provide an orbital home for astronauts to remain in space for months at a time.

The *Skylab* mission almost ended before it began. The unmanned *Saturn 5* started climbing into orbit on May 14, 1973. Excessive vibrations loosened a protective micrometeoroid and thermal shield. It tore away in the air blast flowing past the speeding rocket. The large winglike arrays started opening, and one was also torn away. Twisted metal from the broken shield caught the second panel and jammed it in a partially open position. The array reached orbit but was unable to deploy.

Mission controllers knew there was trouble when the electricity levels on the station were much lower than they should have been, and the internal temperature was rising dangerously. To protect the station while a plan for saving it was conceived, *Skylab* was commanded to face away from the Sun.

On May 25, the first *Skylab* crew arrived in orbit. After flying around the station to survey the damage, they docked and went inside. During the 28 days of their stay, Charles Conrad Jr., Paul Weitz, and Joseph Kerwin opened a hatch and placed a reflective nylon and aluminum parasol over the damaged heat shield area to cool the station. On another space walk, the crew used a cutting tool to cut away the twisted metal holding the remaining array. With a little nudging, the array sprung open, and desperately needed elec-

48

tricity began flowing into the station. The spacewalking astronauts had saved *Skylab*. Two more crews eventually arrived at the station. The second stayed 59 days, and the final crew 84 days. The *Skylab* program demonstrated that humans could live and work in space for extended periods.

Right: *Skylab* crew member Joseph P. Kerwin clears away cables and tubing from the damaged solar array panel. After the repairs, the solar panel deployed fully and was operational. Below: *Skylab*, repaired. The solar array panel has been fixed (lower right), and a piece of nylon and aluminum material has been stretched over the damaged heat shield.

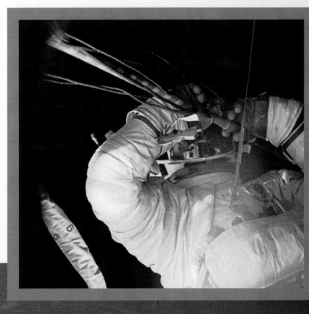

THE WORK OF SPACE TRAVELERS

Early astronauts and cosmonauts spent most of their time in space testing their spacecraft and perfecting skills such as eating, drinking, sleeping, and going to the bathroom. An orbit is a controlled freefall in which the astronauts and all objects on board the spacecraft lose the effects of gravity. Doing simple things on Earth is a challenge in space. You can't just lay a pen down on a tabletop and expect to find it there later. You can't pour yourself a drink of water because water doesn't pour in Earth orbit.

Today's space travelers know how to take care of the necessities because of the lessons learned by all who had flown in space before them. Instead, they busy themselves with scientific research such as studying living things, conducting chemical experiments, and growing protein crystals in a laboratory in which there is no up or down. They also spend much time observing the land passing below. The research they do is designed by scientists on Earth who collect the data and spend months or years analyzing it. In time, enough will be learned to produce new products such as powerful new drugs for curing disease.

Space Shuttle 51L

Whenever something terrible happens, finger-pointing, accusations, conspiracy theories, and charges usually follow. On January 28, 1986, President Ronald Reagan was going to make his State of the Union address. Like all presidents, he wanted to speak of great things. Had all gone well, he could have spoken about the first teacher being launched into space to conduct lessons to thousands of classrooms from Earth orbit. In another view, NASA had been promoting its concept of routine space travel. Already, there had been three delays in launching the Space Shuttle 51L *Challenger*. NASA was condemned by the news media for its inability to reach space on time. In still another view, the teacher member of the crew was to conduct the live lessons from space on the fourth day of the mission. Another delay would cause the lessons to be presented on a Sunday, when schools were closed. Which of these or other theories is correct is hard to know. Most likely, it was a combination of many things that made NASA push ahead with the launch.

Conditions for the launch of the Space Shuttle *Challenger* were not good. Launchpad thermometers read 36 degrees Fahrenheit (2 degrees Celsius), 15 degrees lower than the coldest day a shuttle had flown before. The low temperatures concerned engineers, who were experts in solid-booster rockets. The boosters are made in tube-shaped segments that are stacked one on top of another. A tongue from the bottom edge of the segment above slips into a groove on the upper edge of the segment below. Rubber O-rings seal the joints to prevent pressure from escaping when the boosters are ignited. On some previous launches, inspections of the recovered boosters revealed that the seals had come close to failing. Lower temperatures, the engineers reasoned, would make the rings stiffer and less likely to do their jobs. Their warnings to NASA went unheeded, and NASA seemed to rush to launch the mission.

At 11:38 A.M., Francis Scobee, Judy Resnick, Ron McNair, Michael Smith, Ellison Onizuka, Gregory Jarvis, and teacher Christa McAuliffe lifted off on a terribly short ride. Seventy-three seconds into the flight and 48,000 feet (14,630 meters) above the Atlantic Ocean, the external tank of the *Challenger* exploded in a massive fireball. The two solid-rocket boosters split off, and zigzagged away trailing smoke.

In the many investigations that later surveyed the wreckage and the videotapes of the launch, a sequence of probable events was pieced together. At the moment of liftoff, the launchpad was coated with ice, and icicles clung to many of the pad's structures. The overnight low temperatures, combined with outgassing of the supercold liquid hydrogen and oxygen fuel in the external tank, chilled the vehicle and pad to below freezing. The rubber O-rings in the solid-rocket boosters were stiff with cold.

Upon liftoff, a tongue of flame, like a blowtorch, shot out from the lower joint on the right solid-rocket booster. The seal had failed. Flames ate through the insulation on the hydrogen end of the external tank and through the support post that held the booster to the tank. When the tank melted through, the booster started wobbling because it was still attached to the upper end of the tank. The nose of the booster slammed a hole in the upper liquid oxygen tank. The liquid oxygen streamed out and met the liquid hydrogen. Some 400,000 gallons (1,514,165 liters) of fuel detonated.

Challenger, January 28, 1986, about 73 seconds after takeoff. At the bottom of the booster, near the exhaust trail, is a bright spot, the flame from the failed O-ring seal.

It was very cold on the morning of the 51L launch. The white column at left is a booster rocket. The O-ring seal is the black line around the booster (bottom left).

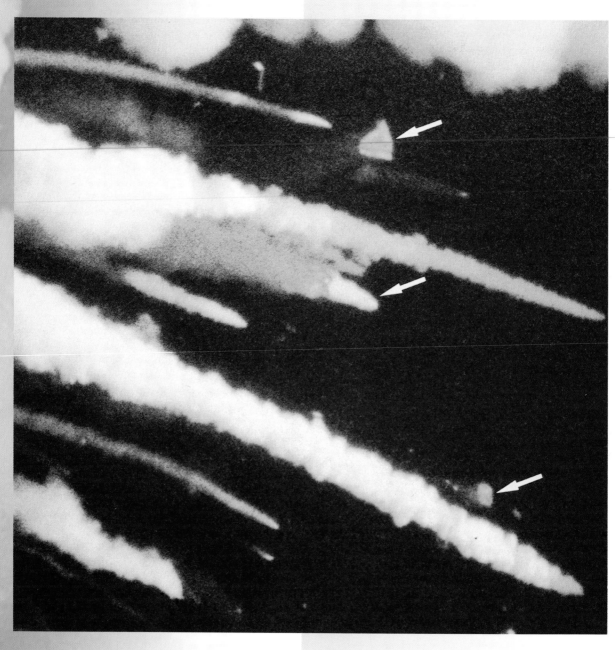

The breakup of the *Challenger*. The left wing (top arrow), main engine (center arrow), and forward fuselage (bottom arrow) fall to the Atlantic Ocean.

The crew of the *Challenger* probably never knew what happened. The cabin they were riding in remained intact. It continued to climb to 65,000 feet (19,810 meters) before tumbling into the ocean two minutes and forty-five seconds after the blast. Doctors have suggested the crew would have been unconscious for their last minutes of life. However, three of four emergency oxygen canisters were manually activated after the explosion. It is possible the crew was awake through the entire fall. They died on impact with the ocean.

Many investigations followed in the wake of the *Challenger* disaster. There was much finger-pointing. Thousands of questions were asked. Congress demanded that NASA fix its problems. Careers were ruined. Most important was the devastation that struck the families of the lost crew.

Two years passed before NASA flew another Space Shuttle. Many improvements were made in the vehicles, including increasing the number of O-rings to three in each booster joint and placing electric heater bands around the joints to keep the rings warm for launch. One question has still not been answered about the *Challenger* disaster. Did NASA learn its lesson this time? It will be many years before the question can be answered.

Fire!

In 1998 the United States and fifteen other nations of the world started orbital construction of the International Space Station. As big as two football fields side by side, the ISS, as it is called, will provide world-class scientific laboratory facilities in space. To get ready for the station construction, the United States and Russia began a series of joint flights into space. Cosmonauts flew on the Space Shuttle, and astronauts flew on the *Mir* space station.

The *Mir* station was launched into space in 1986. It was a series of interconnected cylinders, solar panels, and docking ports. Cosmonauts lived and worked on the station for long periods, exceeding a year in space in some cases. A string of U.S. astronauts visited *Mir*. Although the station was functional, the astronauts noted that it was wearing out and much of their time

in orbit was spent maintaining and repairing systems. During Jerry Linenger's stay, conditions got progressively worse.

Linenger arrived at *Mir* on board the Space Shuttle *Atlantis*. Three astronauts had already done a tour of duty on the station. Astronaut John Blaha was waiting on board *Mir* to greet Linenger. After showing Linenger the *Mir* "ropes," Blaha returned to Earth on board the *Atlantis*. Linenger remained on *Mir* for four months until he was replaced by Michael C. Foale.

Although *Mir* was designed for permanent crews of three, periodically the number increased when visitors and replacement crews arrived. It was just after dinner, during a period of overlapping crews, that one of the cosmonauts was performing a routine activity. Sasha Lazutkin drifted down a tunnel to replace a canister that provides oxygen to the station. The canister was filled with a slurry of chemicals that give off oxygen when activated. With six people on board, extra oxygen had to be provided for breathing. Replacing the canister, called a "candle," was a job that was done three times a day.

One of the oxygen canisters on board *Mir*

The Soviet space station *Mir* was in orbit until March 2001.

At first, the canister started working properly, but then Lazutkin was startled by a small orange flame and sparks coming from the unit. In no time the flames grew, and *Mir* emergency alarms began blaring. The situation was critical. The flames shot out like a small volcano. They spread 12 inches (30 centimeters) across and extended out about 3 feet (1 meter), with sparks coming out the end. Even worse, globs of molten metal were forming. Unless brought under control, the flames could melt through *Mir*'s aluminum walls and release its entire air supply. The crew would be dead in seconds.

Dense black smoke was filling the station, and the crew rushed to put on oxygen masks. Some of the masks malfunctioned, and others had to be used. It took several fire extinguishers before the fire was put out. The crew barely survived. For the next several days, the crew wore masks as they cleaned the soot from inside the station. In microgravity anything not cleaned up would be deposited inside their lungs.

Mir Collision

Jerry Linenger was relieved to be replaced on *Mir* in May. Michael Foale took over the American slot on *Mir*. He had his own problems to face.

Less than a month on board *Mir*, Foale observed the cosmonauts perform a practice docking maneuver with a spent *Progress* resupply spacecraft. Normally, the *Progress* docked to the station with an autopilot system. The cosmonauts were testing a manual system that involved cameras and television screens. Using radio control, the *Progress* would be flown to the docking port by the cosmonaut in control.

The manual docking system had been troublesome, and the first test resulted in a near collision of the *Progress* and *Mir*. By luck, *Progress* whipped by *Mir* without colliding. The second trial was not so blessed. More problems plagued the test, and this time *Progress* collided with *Mir*. The collision rocked the space station. The crew felt a heavy jolt and heard metal crushing. A small hole was created in one of the modules, and air began rushing

Mir, after the collision with *Progress*

WHAT ARE THE CHANCES?

After the *Challenger* disaster, safety experts reviewed the entire Space Shuttle program. They wanted to assess the risk of future shuttle flights, and one estimate put the chances of a Space Shuttle launching into space and returning to Earth at 96 percent. Traveling into space is not safe, but then all forms of transportation have some inherent risk. An estimate of 96 sounded good, but was it?

On a test in school, a score of 96 is a solid A, meaning the test taker's performance is excellent. However, a score of 96 for a transportation system is definitely an F minus. Think of airplanes for a moment and one airport in particular, Chicago's O'Hare Field. If airplanes were 96 percent safe, an average of four airplanes would crash at O'Hare Field every hour, twenty-four hours a day. The public wouldn't stand for that kind of performance. The only reason a 96 score has been acceptable in the space program is that there aren't that many flights. Since the first Space Shuttle flight in 1981, more than a hundred have been launched. Only one shuttle has gone down during that time. NASA is doing better than expected, but spaceflight is still risky.

Following the investigation of the *Challenger* disaster, NASA began a massive effort to improve or replace parts of the Space Shuttle system that could cause trouble. The solid-rocket booster joints were improved. The external tank was strengthened. Improved navigation and other controls have been installed. NASA has announced that when all Space Shuttles are fully upgraded by the year 2005, such travel will become twice as safe as it is today. That means that NASA still could lose an average of two shuttles in every hundred flights.

out. The rate of air loss was so great that the station would be uninhabitable in 22 minutes. Unless the crew evacuated into a *Soyuz* spacecraft attached to the station, they would surely die.

The crew was prepared to evacuate but not without a fight. The general site of the leak was determined, and a battle plan was formulated. With their ears popping from lowering air pressure, the crew closed the hatch to the damaged module. It wasn't an easy job. *Mir* was an old station. There were many wires running through the hatch. The wires had to be removed before the hatch could be closed. However, the crew couldn't just cut through the wires without being electrocuted by some of them. The electricity had to be shut off first. The crew worked fast and efficiently and finally cleared the hatch. They shoved the hatch closed, and immediately the air pressure in the remaining station stabilized. The crew had saved *Mir*.

TROUBLE WITH ROBOT SPACECRAFT

Space disasters are not limited to manned space missions. Unmanned missions have had their share of troubles as well. On the positive side, nobody gets hurt. On the negative side, time, money, and the hoped-for scientific data are lost.

Sending spacecraft to study the planet Mars has been rough. Nineteen spacecraft to Mars have failed, and only twelve have succeeded. The successes have been wonderful, like the *Mariner 9, Viking,* and *Pathfinder/Sojourner* missions. The failures have hurt. In 1992 the billion-dollar *Mars Observer* spacecraft disappeared as it tried to orbit Mars. It is believed to have exploded. More recently, the *Mars Climate Orbiter* spacecraft failed because of a simple mathematics error involving British and metric measurement conversions. The *Mars Polar Lander* that followed a few months later failed as it tried to land.

An even more disastrous failure turned out all right in time. In 1990, NASA launched the Hubble Space Telescope. The spacecraft was designed to see seven times deeper into space than any ground-based telescope. It was to have opened a "new window" into the universe. Things didn't quite work out that way.

During the grinding and polishing of the telescope's mirror, a mistake was made. The NASA managers were not experienced enough with telescope mirrors to realize that the error had been made by the mirror company. They did not require the proper tests that would have detected the problem. The error was ever so slight, but it was enough to ensure that the images of deep-space objects were out of focus.

When it was discovered, there was a huge public uproar. It was a tragic but not hopeless situation. Careful study of the images radioed down to Earth helped scientists and engineers pinpoint the problem. The mirror was slightly more rounded than it should have been. The error was equivalent to one-fiftieth the thickness of a human hair.

A repair strategy was formulated. The Hubble Space Telescope was designed so that instruments could be replaced as needed. Three and a half years after the telescope was launched by the Space Shuttle, another shuttle returned to it. During five space walks, crew members replaced instruments and did general servicing work on the

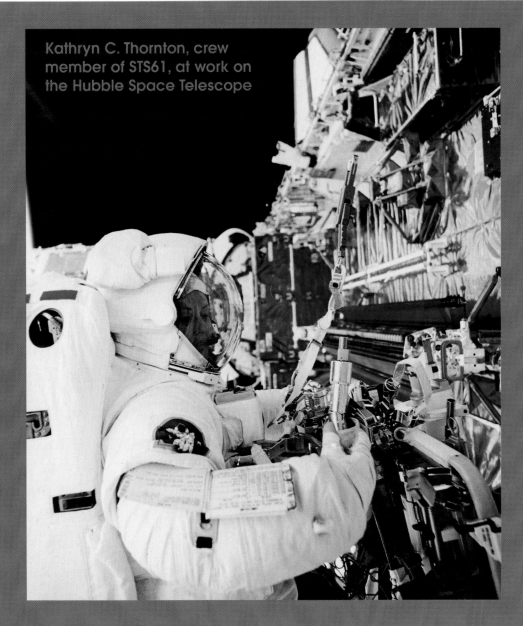

Kathryn C. Thornton, crew member of STS61, at work on the Hubble Space Telescope

telescope. The focus problem was fixed by giving the Hubble Space Telescope a pair of glasses. Corrective lenses were installed into the telescope's light path, which brought the light to a fine focus.

Since the repair mission, the Hubble Space Telescope has been functioning so well that most people have forgotten its early problems. It has been a discovery machine opening many of the deepest parts of the universe to observation.

Chapter four

CARRYING
CARRYING
THE FIRE
THE FIRE

Space exploration has only begun. The farthest humans have traveled is the Moon. There is a whole solar system to explore. In the next few decades, astronauts will probably return to the Moon to establish a permanent base there. They will face many challenges and dangers. One challenge is to supply their base with oxygen, water, fuel, electricity, and food. Nearly everything they need can be found on the Moon, and greenhouses can be built to grow food. Supplies can be brought from Earth, but transporting them will be expensive.

The Moon will be an unforgiving environment. There is no atmosphere, and astronauts must live inside shells or fully enclosed space suits. Temperatures will shift by hundreds of degrees just by crossing from sunlight into shade. Their living structures must protect them from meteorite impacts and deadly radiation from the Sun. Because of low gravity, stumbling and falling on the Moon won't be as painful as on Earth. However, the lower gravity, one-sixth that of Earth gravity, will encourage muscles and bones to go soft. Heavy daily exercise will be a necessity.

After the Moon comes Mars. Getting to Mars will be the problem. A one-way trip could take between three and six months. Delivering supplies to Mars will be a major nightmare. The temperature on Mars is milder than on the Moon but still harsh. Gravity is a bit higher, and the atmosphere is thin. The big problem is that you can't run home if disaster strikes. On Mars you either handle it yourself or die. In the future, astronauts on the Moon and on Mars will be well prepared and have equipment to do their jobs in reasonable safety. However, as in every other venture in space, the things that you don't imagine and don't prepare for are the ones that will get you.

Why Go?

As humans expand the sphere of life out to the Moon and the other planets, the dangers to future astronauts will increase. What happens when your oxygen system fails and you have only a two-day supply before you run out? If you are orbiting Earth, you come down. If you are heading out toward Mars, you don't have enough fuel to turn your spaceship around and head back. You need Mars's gravity to swing you back toward Earth and several months to actually reach home. That's just one possible emergency out of thousands that could present themselves.

Knowing the many dangers and the chances of injury or death, why do highly trained astronauts still venture into space? A long time ago, a mountain climber was asked why he climbed a mountain. His reply was "Because it's there." This answer has been repeated by mountain climbers and adventure seekers ever since. To people who have never climbed a mountain, the answer is as mysterious as the act of climbing the mountain.

You can ask astronauts a similar question: "Why do you go into space?" You probably won't hear them say "Because it's there." Astronauts are trained in many things, including public relations. They will tell you about the importance of exploring space and conducting science experiments for the good of the country. They will tell you that space exploration inspires young minds to study science and math at school. They will tell you that the results of their experiments could lead to a cure for AIDS, cancer, or osteoporosis. They will tell you about how we can learn about our home planet from space and how this information will lead to protecting its environment for future generations.

Certainly, all those reasons are good ones for going into space, but there are others that are harder to put into words. Humans are born with a tremendous sense of curiosity. Although many adults seem to lose that sense as they get older and bogged down with the business of living, it is still there. Curiosity in humans is aimed not only toward seeing the unknown but also at understanding it.

Because of human curiosity, humans have survived and populated nearly the entire land surface of Earth. Humans have also probed the bottom of the oceans and traveled to the Moon. Spacecraft, constructed by humans, have traveled farther out into space than the planet Pluto, and they will continue to explore the realm of the stars. Humans have explored the mysteries of life and the inner workings of the atom. Not all of our curiosity has led to good. There have been wars and environmental destruction, but the long-term path of human exploration generally has been good.

While many people may choose to lead lives of quiet safety, humanity only thrives when it lives on the edge of a frontier. A hundred years ago, humans first began to fly powered airplanes. The airplanes were unstable, didn't go very far, and were hard to control, uncomfortable, and dangerous. Adventurers still took to the air. They seemed to crash as often as they flew safely. Every airplane crash taught airplane designers something new. Airplanes gradually became safer. Eventually, airplanes brought the nations of the world closer together. Now, the beginning of the twenty-first century, millions of people fly safely in airplanes every day. We can thank tens of thousands of experimenters, engineers, technicians, and pilots who gave their careers and sometimes their lives to conquer the frontier of flight.

Although more than 40 years have passed since the first human orbited Earth, spaceflight is still in its infancy. It is much harder to fly into space than to fly through the air. Hundreds of thousands of people work to make spaceflight possible for a few people. The dangers still abound, but astronauts eagerly line up to fly. Instead of a few dozen people flying into space every year, soon hundreds will begin flying, and then thousands.

In spite of the dangers, every flight into space, whether it ends well or not, teaches us something. It can be argued that we learn more from failure than from success. Each failure takes us a step closer to the stars.

It is difficult to write a book about space disasters without giving the false impression that space exploration is just one long line of misfortunes and failures. To be sure, there have been many of them, but they are not restricted to space exploration. It's not hard to find colossal calamities. For example, look at what happened to the Donner Party crossing the Sierra Nevada mountains or the maiden voyage of the *Titanic*.

At least a dozen astronauts and cosmonauts have lost their lives trying to get to space or to return home. Failures and tragedies, yes. What about the successes? There have been many. Taking the United States space program as the example, there were six safe *Mercury* flights. Ten *Gemini* flights returned safely. Counting the return of *Apollo 13*, there were eleven flights in the Moon program. The *Skylab* program featured three flights and *Apollo-Soyuz*, one. Finally, there have been more than a hundred flights of the Space Shuttle. We can't ignore the successes.

Glossary

Airlock a pair of doors with a chamber between them that permit astronauts to venture outside their spacecraft without losing all the air inside the cabin

Astronauts human space travelers who fly into space on American space vehicles

Attitude control small rockets on a spacecraft that enable it to change the direction it is pointing in orbit

Capsule a spacecraft for human or animal passengers that is sphere- or bell-shaped

Cosmonauts the Russian name for human space travelers

International Space Station the space station currently under construction by the United States and 15 other nations around the world

Orbiter the delta-winged spaceship that is a part of the Space Shuttle transportation system

Reentry passing from space back into Earth's atmosphere

Retrofire a firing of a rocket engine in the opposite direction a spacecraft is moving to slow the spacecraft so that it can reenter the atmosphere and land on Earth

Satellite a natural body or machine that orbits a planet or a moon

Space Shuttle spacecraft used by the United States for carrying astronauts into space

Further Reading

Burrough, B., *Dragon Fly: NASA and the Crisis Aboard Mir*, New York: HarperCollins, 1998.

Burrows, W., *This New Ocean: The Story of the First Space Age*, New York: Modern Library, 1998.

Crouch, T., *Aiming for the Stars: The Dreamers and Doers of the Space Age*, Washington: Smithsonian Institution Press, 1999.

Linenger, J., *Off the Planet, Surviving Five Perilous Months Aboard the Space Station* Mir, New York: McGraw-Hill, 2000.

Lovell, J., and J. Kluger, *Lost Moon: The Perilous Voyage of* Apollo 13, Boston: Houghton Mifflin, 1994.

Internet Sites for Information About NASA Spaceflight Missions

NASA Homepage

http://www.nasa.gov

NASA Johnson Space Center Homepage

http://www.jsc.nasa.gov

International Space Station

http://spaceflight.nasa.gov/station

Index